Around & About
ST. AUSTELL
1880 ~ 1930
"A Glimpse into Yesteryear"

By Peter Bray

ACKNOWLEDGMENTS
Ada Whale of Polgooth, Marilyn Crotty of St. Austell and E V Thompson, whose combined assistance and co-operation has made this book possible.

ISBN 1 871273 05 6

Published by CORRAN PUBLICATIONS, St. Ewe, Cornwall   Telephone: (0726) 842072
Printed by Francis Antony Limited, St. Austell
© 1987

Introduction

For more than twenty-five years my all-absorbing hobby has been the collection of Cornish postcards, covering the reigns of Victoria, Edward VII and George V.

I have frequently exhibited postcards from my collection in the St. Austell area and the interest shown in them has prompted me to put a selection of cards into pictorial book form.

In this modest book I have selected scenes of St. Austell and the surrounding district that are recognisable today and for many readers I hope it will provide happy memories of yesteryear.

Postcards produced in this part of Cornwall were well known for the high photographic standard they set and we were fortunate to have living here such photographers as the silver medal winning S. Dalby-Smith, W. Lyons, F.C. Elger, H. Gibbs, W. Orchard, E.J. Russell, J.H. Coath and many others.

Over the years I have derived a great deal of pleasure from my hobby and it is my hope that some of this pleasure may be shared with those who read this book.

Peter Bray

Contents

Foreword by E V Thompson	3
St. Austell and Mount Charles	3 - 12
Charlestown	13 - 17
St. Blazey and Par	18 - 23
Sticker, Trelowth and Polgooth	24 - 25
China Clay and Sport	26 - 29
Local Bands	30
Bugle	31 - 32

Foreword

It always pleases me to see a part of our fascinating history preserved for those who come after us and a pictorial record, such as this, somehow manages to bring the past much closer to the present.

Peter Bray is well-known in the area for his talks and slide-shows, illustrating through his hobby details of earlier days in Cornwall. More recently, he has begun re-producing, enlarging and framing his postcards in a commercial venture and they now adorn many homes throughout the country.

Peter has put together postcards showing how the area about St. Austell has changed during the last 100 years and I predict that, during the next few years, there will be a demand for many such books depicting other parts of Cornwall. I certainly hope so. Peter Bray's postcards are a veritable treasure-house of Cornish history and of interest to visitors and residents alike.

E.V. Thompson

WEST END, ST. AUSTELL.

WEST END, ST. AUSTELL
The message on the reverse of this card reads, "have you forgotten this street and do you see Mr Reed the postman looking out the doorway. Best wishes for a Happy Xmas and New Year from Kate". It is addressed to Mr. W. Common, 24 Stanley Street, Sydenham, Christchurch, New Zealand.

CHURCH STREET AND CHURCH, ST. AUSTELL
July 1914. The White Hart Hotel is in the foreground. The driver of the stationary clay wagon may be inside, but it is more likely he was assisting another wagon to ascend the steep hill. Clay wagons would take this route between 'Clay country' and the port of Charlestown.

WEST HILL AND TRURO ROAD, ST. AUSTELL
This fascinating building was a footwear shop occupied first by Rickards and then Treloars and later by Goodenough between the years 1888 to 1965. It has now been demolished.

BODMIN ROAD AND TRENANCE VIADUCT, ST. AUSTELL
Another of the cards addressed to W. Common in New Zealand. This is the 'new' Trenance Viaduct, built of local granite to replace the original trestle-type viaduct, the supports of which are still in place.

ST. AUSTELL FEAST, 1910. Part of the Feast Week activities, this happy group was photographed at Trevarrick by H. Gibbs of Slades.

TRURO ROAD, ST. AUSTELL.
An interesting photograph of the Assembly Rooms, venue for the Magistrates' Court, auctions, boxing matches, operas, dancing and many other functions. The postcard was posted in 1911. Addressed to Mrs. T. Buckthought of Barnstaple, the sender promises to pay her a visit if she has any money left after paying her doctor's bills.

MARKET HOUSE, FORE STREET, ST. AUSTELL
An early 1900's card produced by W.H. Smith. This impressive old structure still serves its original purpose. At the turn of the century farmers' wives would bring produce in and display it for sale on the upper floor.

RAILWAY STATION, ST. AUSTELL.
A busy day at around the turn of the century. A nostalgic scene to delight all G.W.R. railway enthusiasts. On the right of the picture are the sidings off Palace Road where clay trucks were shunted before being taken to Fowey.

THE DECORATIVE PREMISES OF MESSRS DONEY & WATTS, MONUMENTAL MASONS, TRURO ROAD, ST. AUSTELL.
This fascinating card, printed by W. Lyons of High Cross Street and posted on 3rd April 1905, was produced as an election 'gimmick', urging voters to choose 'Doney, No.1 on the Ballot Paper'. The statue in the alcove above the shop front was in position until only a few years ago. Where is it now?

FOUNTAIN AT ST. AUSTELL.
Another of Doney & Watts cards. This fascinating structure stands outside the church and was designed and erected by Messrs. Doney in 1890 to provide welcome refreshment for thirsty travellers and animals. The Doney firm was later taken over by Williams & Giles of Park Road.

WORTHINGTON, EAST HILL, ST. AUSTELL.
This card was an advertising 'giveaway' in an age when ready-made suits were sold for 18/6d (93p) and tailor-made suits could be made for 37/6d (£1.88p). In addition, the shop provided entertainment for children who would watch the tailors at work through the small windows.

WATERING HILL, ST. AUSTELL
This card was posted in Newlyn on 1st October 1910. The hill was so-named for the stream which crossed the road and where cattle and horses being driven to market drank and were rested. The road is now Alexandra Road and the Capitol Theatre, built in the 1920's is at the bottom of the hill.

MOUNT CHARLES.
No traffic lights to stop the traffic when this photograph was taken although the photographer seems to have succeeded equally well. Note the candle-lantern on the side of the baker's wagon and the early bicycle.

WESLEYAN CHURCH AND VICTORIA ROAD, MT. CHARLES.
Issued by W.H. Smith about 1910, the card shows the Victoria Road Chapel which was given over to Belgian refugees in October, 1914 and not re-occupied until January 1916.

CHARLESTOWN ROAD, ST. AUSTELL
Angle House, Mount Charles, situated between the busy Charlestown Road and Bray's Row was demolished in recent years to make way for the roundabout at the Eastern end of the by-pass.

CHARLESTOWN DOCK.
Vessels loading China clay in the busy little inner harbour in January 1912. Coal was brought to Charlestown and after they had been unloaded and their holds thoroughly cleaned they would leave with a load of china clay on the next tide and so avoid further harbour dues.

CHARLESTOWN DOCKS, NR. ST. AUSTELL.
The outer harbour at high tide, with the old dock gates closed. The docks were at their busiest in the early part of this century. Less busy today they have become popular with film-makers.

CHARLESTOWN DOCK.
An unusual aerial view of Charlestown showing steam and sail side-by-side in the harbour. Horse-drawn clay wagons are queueing to load the ships and one wonders what type of aircraft was used to obtain this photograph.

CHARABANC DAYS!
A photograph to bring joy to the heart of the collector. St.Austell railway station in the early part of this century with a vintage charabanc — and see the number plate of the old, solid-tyre car!

COULD THIS BE A BANDSMEN'S OUTING?
At least they have time to pose for a passing photographer. The charabanc is believed to be Vic Walters' "The Bluebird".

This superb photograph is more than a hundred years old. Showing St. Austell's West End and Tidy's Corner, it was taken by W. Orchard of 8, High Cross Street. There is a wealth of interest for local historians here. The 1700's 'Bell House' became Tidy's tobacconist and sports shop and later, Mr. John's. The West End Post Office moved across the street to become part of Reeds Refreshment House.

Mr. Nancollas, Registrar of Births and Deaths moved to the other end of Fore Street. Messrs Best also moved farther along the street and their old premises became 'Frost's music and pram shop'. G. Hawkes' stables, on the right, were demolished in 1888 to make way for the new Liberal Club.

STATION ROAD, ST. BLAZEY.
A Dalby-Smith card of about 1910. Only marginally wider today, this peaceful street is a frustrating and busy spot for modern-day motorists.

HOUSE WHERE DENCH THE ST. BLAZEY MANIAC DEFIED THE POLICE is the fascinating caption on this 1910 postcard. Mr. Dench maimed at least one policeman with a shotgun from this long-demolished house.

ST. BLAZEY MANIAC'S VICTIM.
A policeman who lost a hand when fired at by 'Maniac' Dench. Dench went berserk after being persistently tormented by local youths and the events of the day made sensational headlines in local newspapers.

ITINERANT MUSICIANS.
This charming postcard of January 1905 depicts a husband and wife team who travelled the district entertaining in public houses and appearing at various functions. After their performance the wife would collect donations, at the same time giving away small sachets of lavender to the ladies. The couple were popular entertainers and were reputed to be 'well-to-do'.

WITH MR. ROWE'S COMPLIMENTS.
This postcard, showing a proud butcher in the doorway of his well-stocked Fore Street, St. Blazey shop was a giveaway advertisement.

ST. BLAZEY 1909.
This Dalby-Smith photograph is of the visit of the then Prince and Princess of Wales (later King George V and Queen Mary) to Cornwall. Residents and visitors alike will no doubt recognise this section of main road. The message on the rear of the postcard reads, "An excellent photo of my bike and a very good back view of me."

PAR STACK WITH 25ft OFF THE TOP.
Prior to this photograph of August 1907, the Par stack dominated the sky-line and served as a landmark for shipping entering Par harbour. The stack was shortened prior to demolition in order that it might fall into the available space without damaging adjacent properties.

PAR HARBOUR, CORNWALL.
As it was in 1909, showing a fascinating line-up of sailing ships. The vessel nearest the camera is being loaded with china clay. The card appears to have been posted by a sailor. Addressed to Mr. J. Reid, Ships Broker in Glasgow, it states that the sender and his ship hopes to be ready to sail from Teignmouth 'next Tuesday' and is dated 22nd October 1909.

PAR GREEN IN MORE TRANQUIL TIMES.
In the photograph may be seen the Cornish Arms public-house and the Gott Memorial Hall. The street has a surprising number of gas-lamps and appears to be popular with traders.

TRELOWTH SUNDAY SCHOOL TEA TREAT.
About 1910. The two men closest to the camera are B. Lawry and E.B. Vian. Does anyone recognise any of the others? Note the delightful millinery on display!

TRELOWTH SUNDAY SCHOOL.
The children proudly display their Sunday School banner. The Territorial Army band waits in the background to lead them back to Trelowth from Sticker village for their saffron bun tea.

SOUTH POLGOOTH, COMMERCE MINE.
In this photograph dated about 1903, miners are shown with their candles and picks, ready to go underground to work.

POLGOOTH MINE AND STAMPS.
Polgooth at the turn of the century was a Methodist village and insisted the mines work a six day week. At midnight on Saturday all the stamp heads had to be 'struck out'. The sudden cessation of the 'stamp lullaby' woke most of the residents and kept them awake. The result was that for twenty-four hours tempers were frayed and quarrels were frequent. At midnight on Sunday the stamps were 'struck in' once more and life returned to normal.

CHINA CLAY WORKS, ST. AUSTELL.
The photograph is by W.T. Cook of Caterham, but it has not been possible to identify the site of the clay workings.

GENERAL VIEW OF A CHINA CLAY WORKS, ST. AUSTELL.
The China Clay industry has expanded tremendously since this photograph was taken at the beginning of the century. Mechanisation and modern techniques have had to keep up with a vast increase in demand. Consequently, many houses and small-holdings have disappeared to make way for Cornwall's premier industry.

CORNISH CLAY PITS, BUGLE.
A 1930 Dalby-Smith postcard showing clay bottoms at Bugle, still at the centre of china clay operations. The pit is criss-crossed with hoses and tramways and littered with the paraphernalia of the china clay industry.

A ST. STEPHENS CLAYWORK.
A clay-pit in production at St. Stephen, not far from St. Austell. The pit with its 'sky-tip' has now achieved fame as the logo used by English China Clays International.

A WINNING TEAM.
The St. Austell Ladies' Hockey Team of 1930. Photograph taken by J.H. Coath of High Cross Street, St. Austell.

TREWOON UNITED A.F.C.
The team of 1923/24 with their trophies. Amateur sport has always enjoyed a good following in Cornwall and Trewoon were a particularly well-supported and successful team.

TREVISCOE BRASS BAND.
This splendid photograph was taken by F.C. Elger of St. Dennis . . . but information about this fine group of men ends here. Does any reader possess details of the band?

ST. DENNIS TEMPERANCE BAND 1908.
Very popular at Sunday School tea treats in their heyday. S.J. Govier travelled from Chacewater to capture the photograph for this postcard.

LAYING FOUNDATION STONES, BUGLE, APRIL 22nd 1908.
The building is now the British Legion Hall in New Street. The numbers in the crowd and their manner of dress would indicate that this was an important and well-attended occasion.

BUGLE, CORNWALL. AUGUST 1918.
While other parts of the world were suffering the devastation of World War I, Bugle retained a tranquility that only time and 'progress' might erode. The postcard, from a holidaymaker at Melbourne Villa in Bugle, passes on the message that the sender is having a nice time and the weather is lovely.

STATION ROAD, BUGLE.
On a busy day in 1917. The Bugle Inn is on the left of the picture. The single storey building on the right was demolished to make way for a terrace of houses.

THE SQUARE, BUGLE.
A similar photograph to above, but progress has left its mark. Posted in August 1928, the sender informs friends with whom she had been staying in Chacewater, that she has arrived home safely.